As New Englanders Played

❧

Martin W. Sandler

The
Globe
Pequot
press

Old Chester Road
Chester, Connecticut 06412

Introduction

All of the photographs in this book were taken with glass plate negatives which were the main medium of photography from the Civil War era to World War I. Taking photographs with the cumbersome, fragile glass plates was not easy. Yet early cameramen and women lugged their bulky cameras and other equipment all over New England. It was less than one hundred years ago. Yet, as the pictures reveal, it was a time different from anything we will ever know.

Turn-of-the-century New Englanders were fascinated with the camera. For they saw in it not only a means of recording a way of life, but they saw in it also a way of achieving immortality. They were a proud people and proudly they posed — with their families, on the move, at work, and at play.

Play was a favorite subject of early photographers. For at the turn of the century New Englanders were just learning to play. The Puritan ethic was deeply entrenched in the region, and from the beginning play was looked upon with suspicion and guilt. But the coming of the Industrial Revolution changed all this. New forms of play and recreation were needed to keep pace with the ever-accelerating tempo of life.

New Englanders responded with typical Yankee adaptability and ingenuity. By the time the period was over, play had become big business throughout the region. And from Camden to Cape Cod, from New Haven to New Bedford, New Englanders were not only learning to play — they were learning to enjoy it as well.

Most of the photographs in this book have never been published before. I discovered many of them on my "photographic detective hunts" in barns, basements, attics, and shops throughout the area. Others come from the wonderful treasure troves at places such as the Society for the Preservation of New England Antiquities and the Vermont Historical Society. All of them were taken by dedicated, talented pioneer photographers — most of them amateurs. They left us a wonderful gift, these photographers. For they gave us the opportunity to journey back to a unique time — a time which made us what we are today.

Marston's Mills, Massachusetts   *Martin W. Sandler*
August 1979

In New England, the Puritan ethic is, from the beginning, planted deep in the Yankee soil. Play and recreation are looked upon with deep suspicion and guilt. Whatever recreation exists is taken not far from the front porch.

Often in the living room or parlor. There are a few quiet, respectable sports.

Waqoit Village, Cape Cod, 1892

Lancaster, Mass., c. 1885

Coventry, Rhode Island, 1881

And one can always find ways to amuse oneself. Or enjoy the company of friends and relatives.

But in New England there is so much to see. And the urge to go *anywhere* to see it is very strong.

In The Vermont Woods, c. 1885

Barnstable, Mass., c. 1880

Sunderland, Mass., 1882

Sunderland, Mass., 1883

Increasingly New Englanders set out to
see the land and the sea around them.

Gay Head Lighthouse, Mass., 1887

In The Maine Woods, 1902

Lake Compounce, Ct., 1901

9

It becomes a family affair, enjoying the unique landmarks of New England.

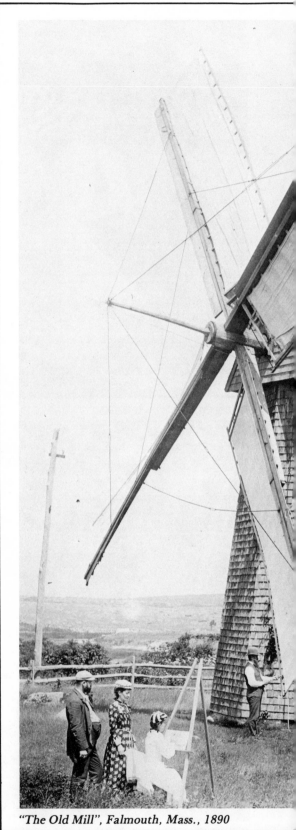

"The Old Mill", Falmouth, Mass., 1890

New Englanders begin to find ways to escape the long hours of work. Clamming on Cape Cod. A Sunday afternoon in the woods. Laughter at the swimming hole. Revelry at the side of the road.

Barnstable, Mass., c. 1880

In The Vermont Woods, c. 1880

In The New Hampshire Woods, 1897

The Connecticut Countryside, 1905

13

The solemnity is still there. You can see it in the faces. But times are changing. The desire to get out and enjoy cannot be denied. And New Englanders find new ways to enjoy their time away from home.

It is still quiet leisure. But with each passing day the feelings of guilt are increasingly put aside. New Englanders take advantage of the land and the sea around them.

Blackstone, Rhode Island, 1898

Mobile Home, The New Hampshire Woods, 1881

Maine Lake, c. 1895

And there *are* some activities which, from the beginning, are acceptable. The country fair, for example, is an early New England institution.

All over New England people flock to the fair.

Bangor, Maine, 1899

Brattleboro, Vermont, c. 1890

Brattleboro, Vermont, c. 1890

The bands play. There are amazing sights to behold.

Amazing indeed!

Lynn, Massachusetts, 1898

Concord, N. H., 1894

And there is another form of amusement which also, from the beginning, is acceptable. The parade.

New Englanders love parades. And there are all types of parades for them to enjoy. Parades for every special occasion. Homecoming Day in Connecticut. A Portugese festival in Massachusetts.

New Haven, Ct., 1902

Hartford, Ct., 1901

New Bedford, Mass., 1898

And there is a very special kind of parade.

New Bedford, Mass., 1892

In every state, in every city, eventually in every town, animals and performers march to the circus grounds as young and old gather to watch.

Times are changing. Changes beyond imagination. But New Englanders will always love their parades. They put tremendous energy into the uniforms, the costumes, the bands, and particularly the floats.

Augusta, Maine, 1898

St. Johnsbury, Vt., c. 1880

North Conway, New Hampshire, c. 1885

Times will soon change. The parade and its pageantry is one of the last vestiges of a simpler New England.

A simpler New England. A time when play most often revolves around things one has rather than things one needs to go out and buy. For children this is particularly true. There is a time, for example, when animal carts of every description are used by many children as an important part of their play. There are donkey carts. Dog carts.

North Conway, New Hampshire, c. 1885

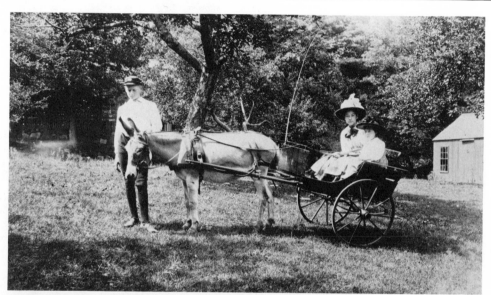

Old Lyme, Ct., c. 1900

Providence, Rhode Island, 1893

Sheep carts. Horse carts.

And, believe it or not, — a rooster cart!

Royalton, Vermont, c. 1885

South Woburn, Mass., 1902

Manchester, New Hampshire, 1899

New England children at play. It is a
different time. The games are simpler.

The toys less costly.

Recess In Vermont, c. 1895

Providence, Rhode Island, 1888   *Flying Top, Camden, Maine, 1887*

The style of dress is different, too. The rules of conduct are much more rigid. But for most children play is an important part of life.

There is another vestige of the simpler life as well. It is the band. Towns, clubs, military organizations all have their own band. The sights and sounds of the musical group is an important part of the New England scene.

Woodstock, Vermont, c. 1885

Lancaster, Mass., c. 1890

Bands bring enjoyment to listener and participant alike.

There are harmony bands, coronet bands, marching bands. Bands of every description.

Burlington, Vt., c. 1890

Orleans, Mass., c. 1885

Franklin, Vt., c. 1890

Hanover, New Hampshire, c. 1885

Proudly they pose — the drummers, the trumpeters. All in their uniforms. All as proud of themselves as they can be.

In New England playing in a band means you belong. And to many no band is more important than that which is made up of family members. From towns and cities all over New England they gather. To rehearse, to perform — to be together and play. A simple pleasure — in a simpler time.

Lancaster, Mass., c. 1890

Weston, Vt., c. 1885

Burlington, Vt., c. 1890

But this is the turn of the century. The times are changing rapidly. The industrial revolution and the growing cities bring about a need for new, more active ways of recreation and play. Recreation to keep pace with the accelerating tempo of life.

New England woods, streams, and lakes become avenues of escape from the toil of the mill, the turmoil of the factory. Hunting clubs are formed. Fishing becomes increasingly popular.

In The Maine Woods, 1901

Massachusetts Gun Club, 1898

Rocky Point, Rhode Island, 1903

New Englanders find camaraderie in the hunt. No animal is too small. Or too big.

It is a chance to prove one's manhood. And one's womanhood as well.

Lancaster, Mass., c. 1890

In The Vermont Woods, c. 1890

Off Cape Cod, c. 1900

In The Maine Woods, 1902

The pace continues to accelerate. Leisure becomes more and more active. And New Englanders find another form of recreation — one destined to become extremely popular.

The bicycle becomes a familiar part of the New England landscape. Cycling clubs are formed everywhere.

In The Berkshires, Massachusetts, 1896

Burlington, Vt., c. 1895

Outside Worcester, Massachusetts, 1887

There are even bicycle bands.

Recreation is becoming more and more active. The faces look less and less guilty. And the New England winter presents an ideal setting for active pursuit of pleasure.

Boston, Mass., 1896

Brattleboro, Vt., c. 1895

Pursuits which involve both men and women.

Montpelier, Vt., c. 1885

New Haven, Ct., 1902

Outside Woodstock, Vt., c. 1890

It is a new active life. More and more people are involved. And the New England landscape provides the perfect setting for it.

The active, sporting life. It is upon them. By the turn of the century New Englanders are involved in sports of all kinds.

Nonombega Park, Newton, Mass., c. 1900

Medford, Mass., 1900

For the relatively well-to-do, there is golf.

And tennis!

Mt. Pleasant House Golf Course, White Mountains, New Hampshire, 1902

Mt. Pleasant House Golf Course, White Mountains, New Hampshire, 1902

New Bedford, Mass., 1897

For everyone there is croquet. A game that can be played by anyone. Men, women and children. Played anywhere. On the lawn — at home — in the mountains.

More and more New Englanders become involved in sports. They are playing in great numbers. And now in even greater numbers they are watching. The desire to escape the office and the factory brings about a new phenomenon — the rise of spectator sports.

Mt. Mansfield, Vt., c. 1880

New Haven, Ct., 1901

New London, Ct., 1903

By the thousands New Englanders fill places like the Yale Bowl, Harvard Stadium, and the Huntington Avenue home grounds of the Boston American League Baseball Club.

And there are events particular to the age. Whenever, for example, there is a balloon ascension or an automobile hill race, a crowd is sure to gather.

New Haven, Ct., c. 1900

Boston, Mass., c. 1900

Lancaster, Mass., c. 1890

Mt. Carmel, Ct., 1905

The age of sports and spectators has arrived. From Maine to Cape Cod the athletes perform; a crowd gathers to watch. New Englanders are truly at play — and they are enjoying it.

There are other things to enjoy as well. It is a remarkable era. An age of invention. And many of the inventions will allow New Englanders to move about and play in ways only dreamed about before.

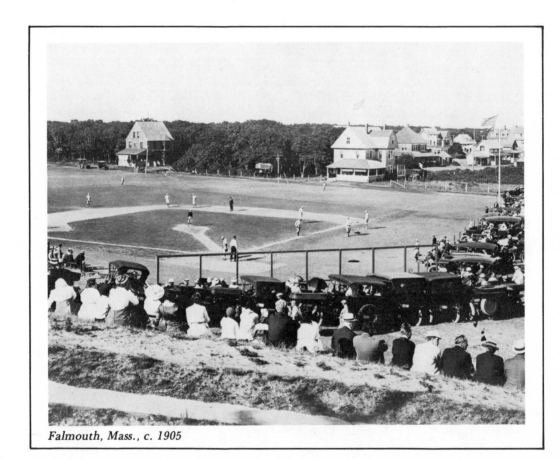

Falmouth, Mass., c. 1905

Oak Bluffs, Mass., c. 1880

In the beginning of the era, it is the horse and the horse and carriage that bring New Englanders to their places of play.

And as play becomes more and more important, another old friend — the sea — also provides a means of recreation.

Lancaster, Mass., c. 1895

Franconia, New Hampshire, 1877

The Maine Coast, c. 1890

From the beginning in New England, the sea has been a vital source of commerce and employment. Now the sea becomes a vital source of recreation and play as well.

Woods Hole, Mass., c. 1890

But even life on the sea is changing. The age of sail is being replaced by the age of steam.

And steam allows New Englanders to travel by sea further and in greater numbers than ever before. A new term is introduced. The era of the excursion is born.

The Rhode Island Coast, 1885

Lake Winnipesaukee, New Hampshire, 1897

New London, Ct., 1893

In America it is the *age* of steam. And New Englanders use it not only for their work but for their recreation as well.

Steam — it heralds the transportation revolution. New ways to move about. New ways to work. New ways to play. One invention begins to dominate the age. It will move more people to more places than any previous invention.

Provincetown, Mass., 1886

Westport, Ct., 1887

In New England, as in other parts of the country, excursions by train become an important part of play. There are particular trains to particular areas.

Some of the "train rides" are unorthodox, to say the least.

Mt. Washington (New Hampshire) Railway, c. 1885

Atop Mt. Washington, New Hampshire, 1887

Sliding Down Mt. Washington (New Hampshire) Railway, 1888

The train brings vacationers to every corner of New England. From Camden to Provincetown, no place is now too far away for a vacation.

And within the cities themselves and into the newly grown suburbs there is another invention of the age. The trolley is another important source of excursion. All over the region, New Englanders ride the trolleys in search of relaxation and pleasure.

Provincetown, Mass., c. 1905

Auburn, Mass., c. 1895

And by the turn of the century there is still another mechanical marvel. It is called the automobile and it will change the way of life for Americans for all time.

The automobile goes places that neither train nor trolley can get to. Increasingly it becomes a major means of recreation.

Pownal, Vermont, c. 1900

Wallingford, Ct., c. 1905

Little Compton, Rhode Island, c. 1910

Entire excursions are planned around the "horseless carriage".

There are automobiles of every description. And for individuals and whole families a ride in the new auto is recreation itself.

White Mountains, New Hampshire, c. 1910

Medford, Mass., 1912

Conway, Mass., 1910

Mountains, lakes, the family cottage
— the automobile makes it possible for
New Englanders to recreate in every
corner of the region.

By the turn of the century it is apparent that New Englanders are living in a remarkable era. An era of incredible change. An era in which more people are seeking more pleasures in more ways than ever thought possible.

Mt. Desert Island, Maine, 1909

Oak Bluffs, Mass., c. 1910

The advances in transportation continue to accelerate the tempo of play and recreation. The trolley companies, for example, in their continuing search for new customers, build amusement parks and beaches at the end of their trolley lines.

Hampton Beach, New Hampshire, 1900

At first New Englanders are cautious about their beaches. It is thought that the sun will ruin their complexion. Also, ministers rail about the morality of men and women swimming in the same ocean. But this is the turn of the century. And in New England, as in the rest of the country, old morals, old ways of life are fast giving way.

New Englanders, who for years have sailed upon the sea or stood on its shores and gazed wistfully out, discover new joys *in* the water.

Narragansett Pier, Rhode Island, 1904

Lighthouse Point Beach, New Haven, Ct., 1904

The beach. Old Orchard, Lighthouse Point, Narragansett Pier, Rye, Rockport, Truro, Wingersheet. All over New England the beach becomes the favorite summer playground.

Lighthouse Point Beach, New Haven, Ct., 1904

One can relax with friends at the beach. One can cavort at the beach.

One can show off new outfits at the beach.

Bailey's Beach, Newport, Rhode Island, 1903

Mystic, Ct., 1906

Maine Coast, 1904

Rhode Island Coast, 1905

One can even be creative at the beach.

The times have changed indeed. New Englanders have not only learned to play — they have learned to enjoy it. And something else is also apparent. Play is not only fun. But with so many people playing it has become big business! Beaches now house not only sand and surf but restaurants, amusements and hotels as well.

The Beach At Swampscott, Mass., 1908

Old Orchard Beach, Maine, c. 1905

The seaside becomes the very symbol of play. For all classes of New Englanders.

Old Orchard Beach, Maine, c. 1905

The amusement parks also grow at an incredible pace. New rides are introduced. New thrills. New entertainment.

Salisbury Beach, Mass., c. 1910

Entertainments to keep pace with the daring new lifestyles of the day.

Play is now an established part of New England life. And soon all of the ingredients — the amusements, the sea, the out-of-doors — are combined in another trademark of the age — the resort.

Rutland, Vermont, 1903

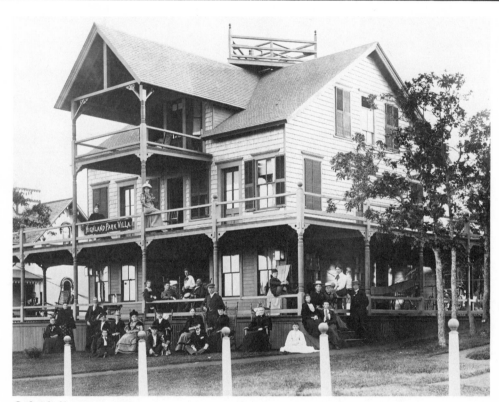

Oak Bluffs, Mass., 1890

The buildings are impressive. The food is ample and good. The air is fresh and clean.

The resort becomes the very symbol of the era. An era which has seen leisure move from the front porch to these very temples of recreation.

White Mountains, New Hampshire, c. 1910

Gloucester, Mass., 1905

For many the guilt associated with leisure has indeed been thrown off. New Englanders have learned to play.

Mt. Washington Hotel, Bretton Woods, NH, c. 1910

Acknowledgments

I wish to thank Mrs. Ellie Reichlin, librarian for the Society for the Preservation of New England Antiquities, for all of the assistance she has given me in the preparation of this book. Also, Mrs. Laura Abbott and Mrs. Mary Pat Johnson of the Vermont Historical Society have been particularly helpful. I am obliged also for the kindness of Ms. Nancy S. Dorr of the Lancaster, Massachusetts, Historical Commission.

My wife, Carol Weiss Sandler, has been, as always, an important part of this project. Finally, I wish to acknowledge the help and encouragement of Robert Wilkerson, President of Globe/Pequot Press. He has become a valuable friend as well as publisher.